California Girl

· · ○●●●●●●○ · · ·

Growing Up in the Great Depression

California Girl

Growing Up in the Great Depression

by
Elsie McCain White

Better Times
PRESS

ISBN-13: 978-0692431047
ISBN-10: 0692431047
ASIN: B00WNDPGFQ

An Original Work
California Girl: Growing Up in the Great Depression is an original work by Elsie May McCain White (15 06 11).

For
My children, grandchildren, great-grandchildren, and all my nieces and nephews.

It was the best of times
It was the worst of times...

Charles Dickens

Contents

· ·‧••❶••‧· ·

What Went Before

California was a golden dream on the western horizon. Its climate, natural resources, and rapidly growing pool of talent drew the ambitious and energetic, eager to make their fortunes or at least a better life than they felt they could build elsewhere. For many, the state delivered on the promise. My father, Columbus Van Buren McCain, certainly never regretted working his way across the U.S. from agrarian Alabama to become a cement contractor in Sunnyvale. He'd come a long way. Southeast of San Francisco and west of San Jose in Santa Clara County, the town was almost as far as he could have traveled without wading in the Pacific Ocean.

Prosperity had come readily to Sunnyvale, still a young community at the time my father brought his family there in the mid-1920s. It was home to the pioneer iron foundry in California. Its manufacturing plants turned out incubators and brooders, camping gear, rubber oil waterproofing for auto tops, and grain separators. Its location on the main line of the Southern Pacific Railroad made it a natural distribution point for fruit grown throughout the region, prompting the location of several large canneries.

Employment opportunities encouraged more and more people to move to Sunnyvale. This, in turn, made necessary the development of consumer businesses and a public environment to serve the town's residents. My father's specialty was sidewalks, and many of the sidewalks in Sunnyvale still bear his mark.

In 1929, Sunnyvale's easy prosperity was about to fade. This book considers the impact of the Great Depression and the World War that followed it. It is not a history but a highly personal selection of memories of what it was like to grow up in that time, when it was possible for even a well-located, bustling town and the hard-working people who lived in it to hit bad times.

California

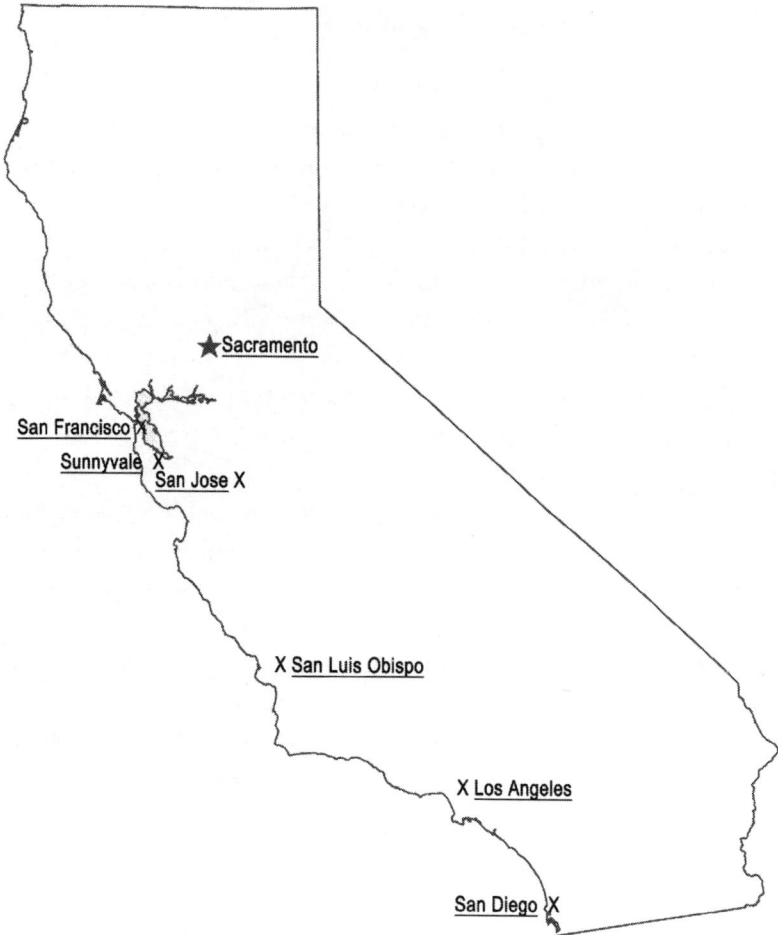

★Sacramento

San Francisco X
Sunnyvale X
San Jose X

X San Luis Obispo

X Los Angeles

San Diego X

Sunnyvale is forty miles southeast of San Francisco and eight miles west of San Jose. It is situated on the main line of the Southern Pacific Railroad, which connects it with much of not only California, but also the rest of the United States.

Sunnyvale in California

Sunnyvale now bills itself as "The Heart of the Silicon Valley," a high-tech mecca. It is home to AMD, Network Appliance, and Yahoo!, among others. NASA Ames Research Center conducts world-class research and development with 2500 employees and an annual budget of almost a billion dollars. Its home, Moffett Federal Airfield, long a joint civil-military airport north of Sunnyvale, is being leased to Google for sixty years according to an announcement made in November 2014. Google plans to use some of the monster hangars for robotics research.

Sunnyvale's population of more than 147,000 includes leaders in technology and academics who make the one-hour drive to Stanford University and other institutions of higher education. It has over 8,000 businesses, twenty-six schools, twenty-one parks, two golf courses, fifty-one tennis courts, 132 sports fields, 315 restaurants, 52 shopping complexes, and ten major hotels, and hosts a wide array of annual events, including: *Art & Wine Festival; Summer Music Series; Hands On The Arts;* and *Downtown Association Holiday Tree Lighting.* Those who can't fill their need for diversion locally can make the drive to San Francisco or the Pacific Ocean, both less than an hour away.

The Sunnyvale about which Elsie McCain White writes, the Sunnyvale of 1929-1945, was a very different place. Blessed with a superb climate and located on the main line of the Southern Pacific Railroad, that Sunnyvale's major industry was the growing, processing, and distribution of fruit. The little town of 3,000 was also home to a certain amount of industry, including the oldest iron foundry in California. The foundry, the Hendy Iron Works, had relocated to the area from San Francisco. There was even an airbase north of town. Until World War II and the coming of big defense expenditures, however, it was fruit that paid most of the bills for much of the population.

In appearance, the Sunnyvale in which Elsie grew up was a pleasant place where streets of simple bungalows gave way to a small number of larger, finer houses occupied by owners of local businesses. The public buildings were modest but attractive. There was one movie theater. One elementary school and one high school served the town. There were sidewalks everywhere (due in large part to the work of Elsie's father Columbus Van

Buren McCain), and parents felt comfortable giving their kids skates to use on them without supervision. There was almost no crime. Neighbors were supportive, not competitive. It sounds idyllic, but even nice towns full of nice people are subject to the laws of economics. The hard times caused by the stock-market crash came to Sunnyvale in the early 1930s and lingered until World War II.

One

·‧∘∘●○●○∘‧·

The Great Depression Begins

I was nine months old when the stock market crashed on 29 October 1929. My arrival in Sunnyvale as the third child of my father's second marriage had been greeted with pleasure; the crash, on the other hand, excited dismay and disbelief. There had been years of national prosperity. Now, everything ground to a halt. Maybe it's just as well we didn't know what was coming, for the crash set off the worst national depression in our history.

I have no memory of the event, but I remember well the effect it had on our little community of 3,000 in the years ahead. People learned to sacrifice and to make do with what they had. Neighbors helped each other whenever they could.

My father, Columbus McCain, was a cement contractor, and after the market crash his work was sporadic. To feed us, he kept chickens and goats, which meant we were well supplied with milk and eggs. Every spring he planted a vegetable garden. He'd grown up on a farm in Alabama, and both liked and knew how to grow vegetables. He said it relaxed him to work with the soil.

My mother, Martha Jane Robinson, was also a hard worker. Her contribution to our family's economic survival was to labor in orchards and processing plants during the fruit seasons. My earliest memory is of her putting me in a baby buggy, and then walking across the fields to a pear shed. My older sisters Marie and Edith walked briskly behind us. At the pear shed Mother placed my buggy at the front of the building, and remained nearby.

At the start of each workday, Mother always gave me a bottle, and I was soon fast asleep. In the middle of the morning I would wake, and begin to cry because it was my feeding time. I had a shrill cry, and there was a young man at the shed who would always shout, "s-i-r-e-n-e, s-i-r-e-n-e!" He probably thought he was being funny, but his shouting made me cry even more. My mother would come over, and give me a bottle of milk. Shortly after, I would be fast asleep.

The shed had a tin roof with lights hanging down over the tables where the women worked. I learned later the women were sizing pears for the canneries in town. A few years ago, I asked my sister Edith what year my mother worked at the pear shed. She looked at me strangely and replied "You can't remember that, why you were just a baby."

I did remember the pear shed, and it is still vivid in my memory.

My next memory is of my mother walking across fields to a patch where she picked strawberries. My sisters and I walked slowly behind her, and I remember I had a hard time keeping up with them. One morning on the way to work, we came upon an irrigation ditch. Mother thought cutting across it would serve as a short cut. My sisters could easily jump its two-foot width, but I was too small to manage the leap. Mother's solution was to hand me to my sister Marie. Everything went well until Marie dropped me in mid-hand-off. Mother quickly rescued me. The temperature was unusually low that morning, and I still remember how cold the water was. Mother did not pick strawberries that day, but took us home as she was worried I would catch a cold from the wet clothes I was wearing.

The following summer, Mother took a job picking prunes at Postmaster Fehey's orchard. My sisters picked prunes alongside her. I was too small and too young to join them, but occasionally I would pick up a prune and put it in a bucket near my mother. At the end of the season, my father gave me three dollars as he wanted me to feel that I had helped. He was a smart man and a good motivator.

We had musical diversion as we worked at the postmaster's. Mrs. Fahey played her radio inside the house loudly enough that we could hear the songs. Those I remember best were *Jack Was A Lonely Cowboy, Red River Valley, Red Wing,* and *That Silver Haired Daddy of Mine.*

Even during the Depression, Sunnyvale was an important fruit distribution and processing center. I remember the two big fruit canneries: Libby, McNeil & Libby; and Schuckl. When I was four years old, my mother started working at Schuckl which was on Fairoaks and Washington Avenues. She walked to work each morning from our home in the six-hundred block of West Washington to Fairoaks, a distance of about one-and-one-half miles. My sisters and I went to the Schuckl day-care center, where we enjoyed playing with other children.

The following year my mother started working for the Libby, McNeil & Libby Cannery. Since it was only a few blocks from our house, it was more convenient for her. To get to work, Mother walked along a beaten path in the orchard that began on Waverly Street and led to Evelyn and Pastoria Avenues. My sisters went to Libby's day care, but Mother hired a woman named Mrs. Pettis to care for me in her home. Mrs. Pettis also took care of a young boy my age, who gave me rides in his wagon. It was fun, but I wanted to be with my sisters. I begged to be allowed to go with them to Libby's day care. After a few weeks, Mother gave in. Unfortunately, the day-care center was not as much fun as I thought it would be. I wished Mrs. Pettis was still taking care of me, but I didn't want to admit it.

There was no certainty as to the day the cannery work would start each season. This posed a notification problem, for not everyone had telephones in those days. Libby's devised a unique system to notify workers when the season would begin. This consisted of a whistle loud enough to be heard across Sunnyvale and into the neighboring town of Mountain View. It would sound in the evening the day before the season started. The system was clever. If the whistle blew seven times, for example, the workers were to report at seven the next morning. This benefited Schuckl Cannery, as the two canneries worked more or less the same hours in the season. Schuckl workers would hear the Libby whistle and assume they were to report.

The workers at the Schuckl Cannery wore blue dresses and blue caps, while the Libby Cannery workers wore white dresses with white caps. Most of the women in Sunnyvale worked at one of the two canneries, as their families needed the extra money to survive. My mother continued working for Libby, McNeil & Libby until 1945. The cannery work was normally ten hours a day, six days a week. It wasn't easy and took a lot out of those who did it, but I never heard my mother complain. She was always thankful for the opportunity to make a little extra money.

Both our parents worked hard and were often exhausted. In the evenings, however, no matter how tired they were, they always took time for us. Sometimes they would sing songs, or read aloud. My father often sang hymns. One hymn I remember particularly was *Bringing in the Sheaves*. For a long time, I thought the song was *Bringing in the Cheese* and pictured a long line of people carrying in a big cheese. I couldn't understand why they would do that. Another song my father sang often was *The Big Rock Candy Mountain*. That I fully understood. I loved that song, and wished I lived by that mountain.

Two

·.₀₀₀₀₀₀₀₀₀₀·.

A Lynching in the Valley

In the early years of the Depression, crime was relatively rare in Santa Clara County. One 1933 criminal event, however, remains famous because it began with a particularly heartless murder and ended with the more-or-less authorized lynching of two men who'd confessed to the crime. Everybody talked about it for years. Although I was not quite five, I recall very well the mood of the community at the time and later.

The victim of the original crime was twenty-two-year-old Brooke Hart, oldest child of Alexander and Nettie Brooke Hart. Alexander, known popularly as "Al," had inherited Leopold Hart and Son Department Store in downtown San Jose from his father, its founder. Hart's specialized in stylish yet reasonably priced clothes. When they could afford it, women like my mother would buy their dresses there.

This was no impersonal business, but a family-run concern. Like his father, Brooke Hart worked at the store even as a boy, and was well known in the community. In 1929, Al sent him to Santa Clara University, just a few miles from Sunnyvale. After graduation, Al made him Assistant Vice President and began to groom him to run the store on his own death or retirement.

As one of the perks of an up-and-coming young businessman, Brooke bought himself a Studebaker Roadster Convertible. Like all young men with a new car, he loved to drive, and he and the car became a familiar sight on San Jose streets. It must have looked as if the world would always be the young heir's for the asking.

All that changed on the afternoon of Thursday, 9 November 1933, when Brooke was kidnapped from the parking lot behind the family store. The kidnappers drove the young executive away in his Studebaker, which they quickly exchanged for another vehicle in a nearby town. They used the second car to drive Brooke to the San Mateo-Hayward Bridge. There, they hit him over the head with a concrete block and tossed him into San Francisco Bay. Since the tide was out and he was unlikely to drown right away, the kidnappers then shot him, killing him at once.

Later that day, the kidnappers phoned the Hart family, demanding $40,000 for Brooke's return. This was the start of a series of botched, misunderstood, delayed, or never-sent communications between kidnappers and the victim's family that ended only with the arrest of Thomas Howard Thurmond on 15 November, six days after Brooke was taken. He'd called the Harts on a tapped phone, and the phone from which he called was only 150 feet from the police station. After hours of interrogation, Thurmond confessed to binding Brooke with wire and tossing him from the bridge into the bay around seven p.m. on the day of the kidnapping. He identified an accomplice, Jack Holmes, who was arrested a few hours later in his room at the California Hotel, which was also near the San Jose police station. Within hours of his arrest, Holmes also confessed.

Lynch threats were sent to the police from the first day of Thurmond and Holmes's arrest and jailing. Initially, there was an attempt to protect the prisoners, as the Santa Clara sheriff moved the two to the Potrero Hill police station in San Francisco.

With the information provided by Thurmond and Holmes, various police forces began searching San Francisco Bay and the surrounding area for any sign of Brooke Hart's body. Several authorities were involved in the investigation and search: the San Jose police; the Santa Clara County Sheriff's office; the U.S. Division of Investigation (later known as the FBI); and police officers from San Mateo County and Alameda County.

Meanwhile, suspects Holmes and Thurmond met with psychiatrists and were reported as planning a defense of "not guilty by reason of insanity." This strategy got a lot of press, which made the two even more hated. The situation wasn't helped when psychiatrists for the state also examined the prisoners and declared them sane. They were back in Santa Clara County by now, and angry crowds began to gather in St. James Park, across from the Santa Clara County Jail.

Talk of lynching grew louder. Santa Clara Sheriff William Emig asked California Governor James Rolph to send the National Guard to protect the prisoners, as did the lawyer hired by the father of Jack Holmes. Rolph refused both requests, saying that he'd instead "pardon the lynchers."

On 26 November, two duck hunters from Redwood City found Brooke Hart's badly decayed body about a mile south of the bridge from which he had been tossed. The discovery triggered an even greater display of hostility toward the suspects. Radio stations announced that a lynching would take place in St. James Park on the night of the 27th. The mob in the park grew steadily until thousands were milling around, muttering threats and vowing action. Clearly, the situation was out of hand, but Governor Rolph and his ally Raymond Cato, head of the California Highway Patrol, were successful in their strategy to make sure the National Guard was not called in to protect either jail or prisoners.

Back at St. James Park, the mob looted a nearby construction site for materials to make a battering ram. Sheriff Emig was aware of what was going on. He knew he didn't have enough officers to stop the mob, and ordered his men to abandon the bottom two floors of the jail where Holmes and Thurmond were being held. When the mob, estimated at anywhere from 3,000 to 10,000, stormed the jail, they were able to take the two prisoners without any opposition. Their last journey wasn't far, just across the street to St. James Park where, without delay, they were hung from a cork elm. In addition to members of the lynch mob, there were reporters and photographers present, and hundreds of photographs were said to have been taken. It was rumored that child movie star Jackie Coogan, friend and classmate of Brooke Hart's at Santa Clara University, was one of those holding the rope used in the lynching.

Governor Rolph had no second thoughts, and praised the lynchings. He even promised to pardon anyone involved. Not all authorities shared his attitude. Alameda County District Attorney Earl Warren fought for prosecution of those responsible for the lynching. Former President Herbert Hoover and recently inaugurated President Franklin D. Roosevelt publicly condemned Rolph's actions.

Jack Holmes's parents sued Rolph for his part in their son's lynching, but he died of a heart attack in 1934 before the case came to trial.

Ultimately, there were a few arrests in connection with the lynchings, but everyone arrested was released with no consequences. Later, the Santa Clara Grand Jury considered the issue, but decided it could not make a finding due to "lack of witnesses."

Three

· · ∘∘●◉●∘∘ · ·

First Grade, At Last

Sunnyvale Elementary School was within walking distance of our house. The front of the school was on McKinley Avenue, while the playground entrance was on Washington Avenue. Above the double doors of the entrance was the sign, SUNNYVALE ELEMENTARY SCHOOL, FOUNDED 1914. In my memory I can still see the lettering. We always entered the school grounds from the playground area on Washington.

I was six years old when I started school. Like other children beginning first grade at the time, I was expected to know the alphabet and to be able to count from one to ten, as well as to write my name. My mother worked with me, and made sure I was proficient in the requirements. My father taught me numerical times tables that a child wasn't required to know so young, but he was extremely proud of my ability to memorize them.

School clothes were always a major undertaking in a household with three girls. A few weeks before the first day, my mother began making dresses for my sisters and me, and she was very creative in her way of going about it. My father always bought chicken feed at Riders Feed Store, which was located on Evelyn Avenue. The chicken feed came in patterned, brightly colored cotton sacks, and my mother used them for dress fabric. First she had to soak off the label. Then she'd remove the chain stitching that held the sack together. Then she'd wash and iron the unstitched sack to get the fabric ready for pattern cutting. To get her patterns, she'd go through the Montgomery Ward or Sears catalogs and spot dresses she thought we'd like and then draw up her own pattern. Sometimes she'd cut patterns from newspapers. She'd pin the pattern to the fabric and cut around it very carefully. With the fabric still turned inside out, she'd sit down at her treadle sewing machine.

The needle was powered by foot action on the treadle, and Mother was so agile at pedaling that you could hear a humming sound throughout the room. She was extremely talented in her sewing ability, and I always felt we had cute clothes.

My first grade teacher was Miss Penner, a motherly woman as well as a superb teacher. Each morning we would start our day by reciting the flag salute, and sometimes we'd sing the song, *Good Morning to You.*

Reading and Writing were probably the most important first-grade topics, and Miss Penner was traditional in her approach. Our reader was the 1930 edition of the *Dick and Jane* books. The books featured Dick, Jane, a dog named Spot, and a cat named Puff. The text incorporated the long-used system of repeating words over and over, which made them easy to learn. Handwriting exercises helped us to learn to write legibly.

Soon, we began to learn to spell. On Monday of each week, Miss Penner gave us five new words, and on Wednesday we had a spelling test. Any word we misspelled on the test, we had to write five times, and a repeat test was given on Friday. I always studied hard, and got one hundred on my spelling tests as long as the teacher graded them. The days of my getting perfect grades vanished, however, when Miss Penner turned the grading over to students.

Each of us had to grade the paper of a classmate, and grading my paper was the responsibility of a girl I'll call Patsy. I don't know if Patsy was jealous or was trying to lower the class average or was just plain mean, but she would change letters in some of my words, which made them wrong. I began to get poor grades, and I did not know what to do. One evening I told my sister Edith about my problem, and she advised me to talk to Miss Penner right away as Patsy needed to stop what she was doing.

The next morning I went to school early and asked to speak to Miss Penner. She heard me out, but did not say anything. I couldn't help wondering if I'd made a mistake in mentioning Patsy's cheating. Then, the next time we had spelling, Miss Penner started walking through the room. As she went up and down the rows, she saw Patsy in the process of changing the letters in my words. She asked her what she was doing.

I'll give Patsy one thing: she was a quick thinker. Even though startled, she quickly replied, "The letters are too light, I am making them darker."

Her ability to think on her feet did her no good. Miss Penner scolded her and made her stay after school the rest of the week. After that, there was no more alteration in my spelling tests, and I was graded on what I had put down. When report cards came out, I received an *Excellent* in Spelling. I was so happy I had followed my sister's advice by talking to my teacher about my problem.

We began Arithmetic each day by playing a game *Going to the Store*. We were given tokens to use when buying apples and oranges. We learned the amount of change we should receive from our purchases. What we learned while playing the store game was a big help when we started having to work addition and subtraction problems on paper.

We had a fifteen-minute recess each day, and there was a wonderful playground for children in grades one through three. The equipment consisted of a large Merry-Go-Round ride that I loved, two swing sets, two sets of bars, and some rings. We always had Physical Education, and we would play games outside except for rainy days when we played organized games in the classroom. Those days were known as "Rainy Day Sessions."

First grade wasn't all work, of course. There were new people to meet and new friends to make. At Sunnyvale Elementary I became acquainted with Jacqueline Stoneberger and Lucille Di Leonardo, two other first-graders who have remained lifelong friends. We lived close to one another, and after school we often played together. The games we played most often were : Annie-Annie Over; Hopscotch; and Jacks.

All in all, first grade was a good experience.

Four

· · ·•••◐◑•••· · ·

Hobo Days

During the drought of the 1930s, there were terrible dust storms in the states of Colorado, Kansas, Oklahoma, New Mexico, and the Panhandle of Texas. In this "Dust Bowl," many people suffered health issues, especially a form of pneumonia that became known as "Dust Pneumonia." Combined with the bad economic times, these climate-related health issues led many from the Dust Bowl to migrate west in the hope of finding work and better health. Because so many Dust Bowl migrants were from Oklahoma, all migrants coming to California at that time became known as "Okies."

Sunnyvale was a popular destination because its fruit canneries and orchards hired seasonal labor. Okies would drive into town with one or two mattresses on top of their cars. The lucky migrants found work in the canneries, while others would work in the orchards picking fruit or in the fruit-drying sheds. The Libby cannery had small cabins it rented reasonably to workers. Fuller's Camp on Coolidge Avenue also had small cabins workers could rent. Often, two couples would rent a cabin and then work different shifts. That way, each couple had its privacy and could rest when its shift ended.

By the time I was in second grade, I became aware that many people were out of work all around the country. The effects of the stock-market crash were felt in every state in the union. Twenty-five percent of the working population was unemployed, and there was no relief in sight. This led to a lot of deprivation. Even in our area, which wasn't hit as hard as many others, there were concerns that some children weren't getting proper nutrition, and the county distributed commodities to schools. The free breakfasts the schools provided were often the most nourishing meals poor children had all day. A few years later, the schools added free lunches for needy children in the district.

Free commodities were also provided by the government to impoverished residents. One of the distribution points was a firehouse on Washington Avenue and Frances Street that we could see from the school playground. People who'd gotten a coupon from Santa Clara County entitling them to the commodities would form long lines at the firehouse. The commodities were a blessing to all those in need but especially to families with children, as the free food meant the difference between having something to eat and being forced to send your youngsters to bed at night hungry.

Hoboes were often seen walking through our town. They came from all over the place, looking for work. They traveled by train. Since Sunnyvale was on the main line of the Southern Pacific, it naturally drew more than its share of the hoboes. Even before the Depression, there were men and women who had hidden in train boxcars for free transportation. During the Depression, they were joined by many more who traveled in this way because they could not afford to pay the fare to get where they needed to go.

Like the Okies, hoboes were drawn by the chance to get seasonal work in the canneries or orchards. Mostly male but with some females mixed in, these were intrepid travelers. They'd start their journey at train depots across the country. They'd wait until the departing train gathered a little speed and then hop into the boxcars. This was highly dangerous, and some hoboes lost arms or legs. Riding the rails in this way was illegal, and hoboes had to be secretive about what they were doing. If they were caught, they could end up in jail.

Most of the hoboes were adults, but more than a few were just kids who'd left home because they felt their families would have more food with them gone and making their own way. Some of these young people had never before been away from home, and were overwhelmed with homesickness.

Many hoboes fed themselves by begging food from the residents of the town where they'd gotten off the train. This could pose a problem, as few people had food to spare in those hard times. Housewives were reduced to feeding their families meals featuring the cheapest possible ingredients prepared creatively, and there was rarely any surplus.

One day after school, I hurried to the kitchen where my mother was making cornbread for dinner. She already had a large pot of soup cooking on the stove. The soup was a testament to her enforced frugality. She'd purchase soup bones at the butcher's for twenty-five cents and then add water and whatever vegetables she had on hand or could be bought cheaply at the store. Once the soup was cooked, she'd remove the bones and give them to the dogs, which was interesting since she and the other housewives would have told the butcher that the bones were for the dogs.

On that particular day, as Mother cooked in the kitchen, my sisters and I were in the living room listening to records on the gramophone when my father came in from work, looking exhausted. He'd put in sidewalks that day, and his hands as well as his clothes were covered in cement. As he went to wash up and change, Mother announced that dinner was almost ready. That was our cue to rush to the kitchen to set the table.

As Daddy entered the kitchen, we heard a knock. Daddy hurried to the front door; and when he returned, a teenager was with him. The newcomer asked if we had any work he could do, as he was hungry and had not eaten for days. He said he would do anything for a little food. My folks did not have any work for him, but they welcomed him to our table. After Daddy said the blessing, we listened to the young man tell about himself. He said his name was Jack, and he was from Texas. He said there was no work where he lived, and that was why he'd hopped the train to look further afield for a job. He was certainly hungry, as he ate two large bowls of stew and several pieces of cornbread. He had good manners. When he left, he shook my father's hand and told my mother how much he had enjoyed the food.

We thought we'd never see Jack again, but a few months later he stopped by our house, looking excited and wanting to talk to our parents.

"I have wonderful news," he said. "The day after I had dinner with you, I got a job working in Mr. Jones's cherry orchard just up the way. When we finished there, I worked in his apricot orchard in

Morgan Hill. I couldn't believe it when he asked me if I would consider working for him year round. He told me he has rheumatism and heart problems and that he sure could use my help. Of course, I said that I would work for him, and he has a small cabin he is letting me live in."

My father congratulated him.

"I feel blessed," Jack said. "It couldn't be any better than that."

Most of those from other places who found work in the area did, like Jack, go to work in orchards or fruit-processing. That's because both required large numbers of people only during certain seasons. That meant that local people who must have full-time employment tried to find work elsewhere before they resorted to fruit growing and processing. That, in turn, meant that opportunities existed for what amounted to transient employees.

It has always been interesting to me that most people who don't have first-hand knowledge of what it takes to grow crops as sensitive as fruit have the idea that this is a "pretty" business.

It *was* beautiful in Santa Clara County when the trees were in blossom, but the weather could quickly turn that beauty into ruin. In the springtime, fruit growers worried nonstop. Anytime they believed the temperature would get near freezing they would put smudge pots out in the orchards. When the smudge pots were lit, the orchard air would be warmed. This prevented the buds and blossoms from freezing, and assured a good crop of fruit.

The smudge pots made life in the neighborhood of the orchards very unpleasant. When they were used in nearby orchards, black soot would creep into our houses. This made it difficult to keep the furniture, walls, and curtains clean. It seemed that everything was covered with soot. We even had black soot in our nostrils, and I can remember all my classmates at school producing grayish black mucous when they coughed or blew their noses. We did not have Kleenex then. Instead, we used cloth handkerchiefs, and I know they were difficult to wash.

The situation was even worse for the men who went into the orchards to light the smudge pots. They would always wear old, but warm clothes. There was no point in wearing anything decent, for the soot often ruined their clothing.

One night when the temperature dipped below thirty degrees, cold enough to cause serious damage to budding trees, my half-sister's son, Aaron went smudging with a friend whose father owned an apricot orchard. Aaron looked pitiful when he came by our house the next morning. There was black soot around his eyes, and nose. His hair was filled with black soot. He said he had ruined his clothes, and then announced he was never going smudging again.

However great the inconveniences caused by the smudge pots, few people complained. Everyone knew that the industry was critical to the national food supply, for Santa Clara County was said to produce two-thirds of the fruit in the United States at that time. Also, a good fruit harvest meant work for both locals and transients.

Five

············

Family in Hard Times

When I look back at the days of hoboes and Okies and meals of bone-based soups, I remember lighter-hearted things as well.

Even when times were at their worst, Christmas was a special time of year for us, as well as for most people in town. We always went to Christmas worship services at church, and our elementary school performed a Christmas program at Sunnyvale City Hall. The program would be presented by the seventh or eighth grade, and the assigned class took great pride in putting on the best possible performance. The evening ended with a prayer by a pastor of one of Sunnyvale's churches. The Christmas program I remember best was **A Christmas Carol** by Charles Dickens. The ghost was very impressive and Scrooge suitably nasty.

Another special holiday school treat some years was when men from Moffett Naval Air Station would bring Christmas presents for the younger students. That was always exciting.

A Christmas I remember particularly was when I was in the third grade. Just before Christmas vacation, we read the story from our literature book about when Mary and Joseph traveled to Bethlehem to pay their taxes and were forced to sleep in the stable where Baby Jesus was born. Everyone took turns reading, and then we sang the song *Away in a Manger*. Afterwards, we sang other songs, and then we began our school party. Some of the mothers made cookies and cupcakes for the class, and we had lemonade to drink. At our school, students in the lower grades could draw the names of their classmates and buy a gift for the person whose name they drew. The gift couldn't cost over twenty cents, and everyone in class participated. My gift was a pretty head scarf, very similar to the one I'd bought for the girl whose name I drew. That day was a lot of fun, but the main reason I remember it is because of what happened at home later.

I heard my sisters open our front door, and my sister Marie walked in dragging a large Christmas tree. Her teacher had asked if anyone wanted a tree. Marie had heard Mother and Dad talking about being so short of money that they would not be able to buy a tree, and so when the teacher repeated the question, she at once piped up that she wanted the tree.

When Mother returned from the store, she was surprised but pleasantly so. She put the groceries away as quickly as possible, and got out her ornaments. She had beautiful glass ornaments, as well as a few crocheted decorations and two sets of Christmas lights. All of us at once set to work decorating the tree, and it was heavenly to see it all lit up. When Dad came in from work, he too was surprised, but I could see he was pleased. That unexpected arrival of the tree had made the Christmas season very special.

On Christmas Eve, we went to bed not knowing whether or not we'd have a present the next day. We knew money was scarce, and we tried not to get our hopes up. Maybe it was a good omen that shortly after midnight, long after our bedtime, we were awakened by the sound of singing from the street. Mother hurried to the window, followed at once by my sisters and me. Outside, we saw carolers, and we were delighted.

The next morning, we went to the tree, pretty sure there wouldn't be a present. To our surprise, we found three beautifully wrapped boxes. Somehow, our parents had managed to get each of us a lovely gold ring set with our birthstone. We loved the rings, but wondered how our parents could afford them, given how hard times were. Years later, we learned that Mother had saved Crystal White Soap wrappers and redeemed them to get our rings. It had taken many bars of soap, which she'd bought when she was working the year before. She stored the unwrapped soap, enough for two years, in a trunk.

That same year, my sisters and I had put our money together to buy Mother and Dad each a new cup and saucer. To get enough, we saved money they'd given us for movies. We were pleased that they seemed happy with their presents, and we heard Mother say, "It's the thought that counts."

The next year, things were a little easier, and we got skates for Christmas. In no time, I learned how to skate, which was useful, as we had sidewalks throughout most of Sunnyvale. Our parents thought skating was good exercise, and we enjoyed the skates very much, especially since many of the sidewalks over which we skated had been laid by our father.

Once present-opening was over, Christmas was family time. Often, my half-sister Eugenia and her son Aaron would come over for Christmas dinner. We always had a wonderful meal. The meat was invariably baked chicken with bread dressing. Mother would start with bread she'd saved, cut into small squares. Then she'd sauté a cup of chopped onion and celery and put it in a bowl with the bread. Then she'd add poultry seasoning or sage, and mix it together. One beaten egg combined with chicken broth was added. The chicken would then be ready to stuff and bake. It took about one-and-one-half hours for the chicken to be completely done. Meanwhile, the rest of the meal was prepared. We usually had cranberry sauce, mashed potatoes, and gravy along with one or two vegetables. My father liked green beans, so that's what we had most of the time. Mother canned beans every summer, so their preparation was basically a matter of being heated up. My sister Marie loved candied sweet potatoes, and she often helped Mother by preparing that part of the meal.

Mother was well-organized, and she'd have everything pretty much ready by the time my half-sister Eugenia arrived, bringing the dinner rolls and the dessert. She liked pumpkin pie, and that is what she brought most of the time.

With all the food on the table, my father would say the blessing, and everybody would dig in. When we finished, we'd sit around the table and talk, mostly about what a fabulous dinner it was. Mother would remark, "I'm glad we have a backyard full of chickens, or else we could never have had baked chicken today." In those days, chicken cost more to buy than other meat. There were many people who simply could not afford to buy it, so it was a real treat.

After dinner, when my sisters and I were old enough, we would wash and dry the dishes, and then we had free time to do whatever we wanted.

We never had Christmas dinner at Eugenia's, as she lived with her family in Fuller's Camp on Coolidge, and their one-bedroom cabin did not have enough room for everybody.

Christmas wasn't the only holiday I enjoyed.

At school, we swapped Valentine cards, and the mother of a classmate would always bring cookies. Easter vacations were a lot like those we had at Christmas, except we did not give gifts. We also never had new Easter dresses unless Mother made them. At Halloween, we went through the neighborhood, trick-or-treating. Most of us couldn't afford costumes but usually wore masks, and I'm afraid we were more serious about the "tricking" part of the event. Woe betide any trash can left in front of a house where we were turned away. At Thanksgiving, my mother did a big chicken-and-dressing dinner with all the trimmings.

The chicken at our holiday dinners would be one of those my father grew for their eggs, which we not only used ourselves but which Dad sold for twenty-five cents a dozen. One time he gave an especially good customer a "Baker's dozen." Unfortunately, the lady was superstitious, and thirteen eggs struck her as a bad omen. She never bought eggs from him again! He would tell the story as an example of never knowing what would come from any act, even one of generosity.

Our dog Muggins, a brownish-red German Shepherd, was another beneficiary of the chickens' efforts. Dad loved dogs, and we always had one or two. Most got along to a lesser or greater degree with the chickens. Muggins, however, would not allow the chickens anywhere near his dog house except for one hen. This particular chicken Muggins allowed to come and go as she pleased. This made Dad suspicious, and he began to keep an eye on what was going on with the unusual activity. It turned out that the chicken was going into the dog house and laying an egg every day, which of course the dog ate. Muggins also liked turnips, which Dad always planted because he liked turnip greens. Unfortunately, he wasn't especially fond of turnips. Often, he'd just cut the greens and leave the turnips in the ground. Muggins would dig a turnip each day and eat it. Why just one, we never knew, but that was his way.

Illness could throw a tight budget into a tailspin. When I was in fourth grade, the doctor — for whom my father had done concrete work in the past — decided my tonsils had to come out. My father didn't hesitate to approve the surgery, but I'm sure he had to pay for it in installments as, like most people then, we had no health insurance.

In bad times, many turned to relatives for help with emergencies. That option wasn't open to us, for we had few family members living in the immediate area. For that matter, there weren't all that many relatives anywhere. My mother, my sisters, and I were our father's second family. His first wife had died, and several of the children from that marriage were much older than my mother, who was thirty-eight years younger than my father. Some of those half-siblings lived in the general area, but we didn't see most of them that often. Because of Daddy's age, both his parents were long dead, buried back in Alabama, and none of his siblings had come west. We didn't know much about the Alabama relatives. About all he said about his childhood was that it was often 110 degrees in the shade and there was no shade! As for my mother, her father had walked out when she was only twelve, and he died before I was born. Her mother was alive but living elsewhere and there was no money for travel. She lived with us briefly when I was a baby, but soon moved, which is why my earliest memory of my maternal grandmother is when I was myself grown up and about to marry.

My most specific memory of the family at the time has to do with my father. Born just before the start of the Civil War, he was sixty-nine when I arrived. He was a wonderful father, and I wouldn't have traded him for any other father I ever met. At the same time, I was aware of the age difference between him and the fathers of my friends, and I worried that he might die. I used to wish that, if anyone had to die first, it would be me, as I couldn't imagine life without him. I think he was probably a kinder, gentler father to me and my sisters than he had been to our older half-siblings. His first wife, by all accounts a very pretty woman, had been a stern, rather temperamental disciplinarian who would instruct him to whip their children on almost any pretext. My mother had a very different ap-

proach, which Dad came to share. They did not whip us; they talked out problems, offering reasoning instead of punishment. In any
event, we loved them so much that we wanted to do what would
please them. That probably kept us from doing a lot of things that
would have called for punishment.

Dad's age showed most in his attitude toward certain kinds of
things that were important to girls. For example, he thought that
wearing lipstick was not "the thing" for nice girls, and I didn't use
it until I was sixteen. Even then, it was never formally allowed. At
my sister Edith's suggestion, I simply started wearing it to see what
would happen. Nothing did, so, from then on, I had red lips like all
the other girls. Another thing he detested was to see shorts on girls.
We never wore shorts at home, and I had to hide a pair I had for
Physical Education at Fremont. Also, he had an absolute dislike of
that "modern" innovation known as hair permanents. None of us,
he announced, were to get perms. In the end, as teenagers, when
times were easier and such things could be afforded, we did pretty
much what we wanted with our hair; we just didn't tell him.

He never said anything. I don't know if he didn't notice our
suddenly redder lips and wavier hairstyles or if he concluded it was a
losing fight and so not worth the bother of talking about. All I know
is that we were like other girls and wanted to do the same kinds of
things with our appearance that they were doing with theirs.

Lipstick, shorts, and perm prohibition or not, he was a terrific
father. I was lucky enough to have him until I was eighteen. I still
miss him.

Six

. . ₀∙₀₀◍◐◍₀₀ . .

Monday Night
at the Movies

My father didn't go to movies, but my mother loved them. Even during the Depression, she economized in other ways so that she could go at least once a month, taking my sisters and me with her. Mother thought that Mae West and W.C. Fields were hilarious, but her favorite movie stars were Jean Harlow and, later, Lana Turner. Truth be told, she liked all sorts of movies. I remember a special favorite was **Gone With the Wind** with Clark Gable and Vivien Leigh.

In addition to the movie trips with Mother, whenever our parents could afford the admission price of a dime for a child's ticket, my sisters and I would go to Saturday-afternoon matinees after we'd completed our chores. Saturday-afternoon movies were always exciting, and we enjoyed watching Flash Gordon or Buck Rogers on the big screen. The space ships in the Flash Gordon movies were very much like the space craft we have today. I enjoyed the Shirley Temple and Jane Withers movies maybe even more, as the stories were more realistic. Often the movies featuring Shirley Temple would bring me to tears, and I would go to the lobby and have a good cry.

One Saturday when my sisters and I were at the movies, it was announced tickets would be given out every Saturday for a month, and then there would be a drawing for a movie projector. That sounded exciting to us and our friends. None of us dreamed we could possibly be lucky enough to win the projector; but when the drawing was held, my sister Marie held the winning ticket. She was overjoyed, especially as several movies were included in the prize. A few days later we invited our friends over to watch the movies with us, and my mother made popcorn for this special occasion.

On Monday nights, Blanco's Sunnyvale Theater gave out pieces of what we now call "Depression Glass." This was glassware manufactured in the Central and Midwestern states in the 1920s and 1930s. It was translucent and came in many colors and patterns. The most popular colors were light green, pink, yellow, pale blue, and amber. Over 100 patterns were made, mostly floral but also geometrical.

At Blanco's, paying the regular adult ticket price of twenty-five cents on Monday night entitled you to whatever piece of glassware was being given out. Mother thought it was wonderful that she could enjoy a good movie and collect beautiful glass dishes at the same time. Like many other housewives, she very much wanted to accumulate a complete set of matching Depression Glass. Luckily, there was more than one way to do this. The glassware was given out not only in movie theaters as a promotional item, but also in Quaker Oats cereal boxes. You could also buy the glass in stores at a very reasonable cost. As a child, I recall seeing a plate in a retail shop for a mere dime.

Mother's preferred color was green, and she attacked the building of a set with perseverance. She bought cereal boxes with a piece of glassware inside. She went to the movies on Monday night to get whatever piece was being given out. She bartered with neighbor women for the right color and pattern. She always loved and valued the Depression Glass, calling the set her "good dishes." We used them only on special occasions.

The movies weren't the only way we entertained ourselves during the Depression, of course. Playing cards at home with friends and neighbors was probably the most popular form of amusement. Favorite card games included bridge, canasta, pinochle, and whist. Some families spent a lot of time playing board games like *Monopoly* and *Scrabble*, both of which were new in the 1930s.

My family enjoyed listening to the radio. My father especially liked the program **Amos and Andy**, which was a popular nightly radio show in the 1930s and 1940s about three black men living in Harlem. The characters in the program were Amos, Andy, and a man called "The King Fish." The King Fish was a schemer who was always trying to swindle Amos and Andy. Rather oddly, black actors did not play the parts. Instead, the two white men who wrote the scripts acted in them as well. My father liked the contrast between the personalities and never missed listening to the program.

I had very different tastes, even as a young child. Several radio shows I enjoyed included *The Lone Ranger*, in which he and Tonto fought outlaws and brought them to justice; and *Jack Armstrong*, an adventure program. Don Ameche played Jack, a popular athlete at Hudson High School, and the show centered around him. His friends were Billy and Betty Fairfield whose uncle, Jim Fairchild, was called Uncle Jim in the series. Uncle Jim was an industrialist who went to exotic countries for business, and Jack and his friends went along. They had many interesting adventures, and all my young friends listened to the show.

Another program I loved was *Our Gal Sunday*. It was the story of an orphan girl who as a young woman marries England's wealthiest, most handsome nobleman. The program always began with "Can this girl from the little mining town in the West find happiness as the wife of a wealthy and titled Englishman?" The series music was *Red River Valley*. This program aired during our school lunch time, and my girl friend Lucille and I would race home to listen to it while we ate a sandwich and then race back to school. I had to run a block and a half further than Lucille, and I got winded!

When I was in the eighth grade and high school, my favorite radio program was *Your Hit Parade*. All the younger set liked this show, probably because we were music mad. Its format was simple. The most popular songs for the past week would be announced, leading up to the revelation of the most popular song. The list was a topic of conversation for me and my classmates the next day, and we did not always agree with the show or with each other as to the popularity of various songs. One song I remember on the list was *The White Cliffs of Dover*, which was popular during World War II. I would always be sure to be home so I did not miss hearing which songs made *Your Hit Parade*.

Another radio show I made sure never to miss was *Inner Sanctum*. The shows opened with a creaking door and creepy organ music. All I had to do was to hear the first notes, and I would settle back to enjoy half an hour of scary storytelling. The host was deliberately hokey, sort of making fun of the spookiness that mystery-horror shows normally tried to produce, but when he got around to the story, it was almost always genuinely scary. Part of what made the show interesting was that it often starred famous horror-film actors, like Boris Karloff and Peter Lorre.

Radio was important to us as entertainment, because we couldn't always afford a movie ticket and television wasn't yet available to the public.

Reading was probably the entertainment I discovered as a child that has been most important in my life. One of my favorite memories is devouring the Nancy Drew series and other books meant to interest girls who cared about more than playing with their dolls. I liked reading so much that I even attempted to get a job at the local library. They had a program where students were given a trial period after which, if they passed muster, they'd then be hired and paid real wages. Books and money, what a combination! I leaped at the chance. Unfortunately, one of the job requirements was that you work until 10 p.m. My father didn't want me walking home alone that late, and said I couldn't work there. I was disappointed, but continued to patronize the library as a reader.

Every book offered visitor privileges to lands and lives otherwise unknown. The public library was my ticket to the world.

Seven

...•••••••...

Summer Vacation

Just like school children of today, I always looked forward to summer vacation. When I was twelve years old, I got my first job, cutting apricots at Wilson's shed located on Pastoria Avenue at the El Camino Highway. My sisters had been working at Wilson's for several summers, and anyone who wanted to work could get hired. My friend Jacqueline had recently moved from Coolidge Avenue to 207 Jackson Avenue which was one-and-one-half miles from where my family lived. She would walk to our house each morning, and then walk with me and my sister Edith to Wilson's. My sister Marie wasn't with us because she was employed full time in San Jose that summer.

The work was simple. We would cut the apricots, take out the seeds, put them in a bin, and then lay the apricots on a large wooden tray. When the tray was full, another tray was stacked on top of it. When we had four trays of apricots, they would be removed and taken by a little railroad car to what was known as the sulfur house. There, sulfur would be lit and the trays would remain overnight. The sulfur treatment of the apricots was necessary, as it kept insects from getting on the fruit while it was drying. After the apricots were taken from the sulfur house and dried, they were removed from the tray, and moved to a packing house where they were packaged for sales.

The foreman at Wilson's was a man named Simon Copas who had recently moved to Sunnyvale. Simon would bring boxes of apricots to us, pour the apricots out on the tray, and punch a ticket each time we finished cutting a box. Simon, his wife Alice, and their son lived in a two-room cabin near the cutting shed. The cabin did not have a bathroom, but there was an outhouse within a few feet of the cabin. The use of the cabin was one of the amenities Simon received in addition to his salary.

Each day at noon, we would stop to eat our lunch. Mrs. Moreno and her children also worked at Wilson's, and they would join us at lunch time. Mrs. Moreno's daughter Mary and my sister Edith were friends at school, and they always kept a conversation going. They not only discussed the subjects they planned on taking in high school, but the plans they had for later in life. Edith wanted to work as a bookkeeper, as she was good at math. Mary was a little undecided about the field she would go into, but she always made good grades, and her mother knew she would do well in whatever profession she chose.

Apricot season was over in about three weeks, and even though we might earn only fifteen dollars or so, it did give us spending money to use as we chose. Most of the time we either bought a pretty dress or just saved the money for going to the movies. Our parents taught us to be frugal with what we earned. Dad used to say, "A bird in the hand is worth two in the bush."

The rest of the summer, while my father and mother were at work, we were given chores to do each day. We had to keep the house clean and do the dishes. Only then could we play with other children in the area. We had friends who lived around the corner on Waverly Street. For several years, their father had worked for Dad, putting in sidewalks in Sunnyvale. We and our friends were always looking for interesting things to do. Once, we thought it would be fun to have a picnic in the middle of the orchard. The next day, we packed sandwiches, making a few extra to share, and our friends brought cookies and a large jar of lemonade. We sat in the middle of the orchard, ate lunch, and had a delightful time. We played the game Simon Says for about an hour, and then sang a few songs. By today's standards of amusement, it sounds basic, but we enjoyed ourselves very much. Whatever we did, we were expected to be at home when our parents returned from work in case they needed us for anything.

When they got home, we would help Mother prepare dinner. In those days, girls always assisted with the preparation of meals. It was part of an upbringing that assumed we would be homemakers and so we should be good at it. After dinner we often played jump rope in the street, and most of the neighbor children were involved. Many times we would sing rhymes while we jumped rope. One rhyme was, "Down by the river, down by the sea." The other rhyme was, "Not last night but the night before." In the evenings we would play games like Hide and Seek or Kick the Can. We were always active, always doing something. I am sure that is why most of the children growing up in that time were not overweight. I knew of only two children who were considered obese.

Eight

· · ·•◦◖◗◦•· · ·

World War II Begins

Most people remember where they were and what they were doing when they got the news of extraordinary events. It was that way with me when I heard on 7 December 1941 about the Japanese attack on Pearl Harbor.

It was a fairly typical Sunday afternoon in our house at 661 Washington Street in Sunnyvale. I was shampooing my hair; my sister Edith was ironing a dress for school the next day; and Marie, my oldest sister, was searching through the want ads of the San Jose paper. Marie's eighteenth birthday was in a couple of weeks, and she was eager to find a real job. She wanted to work as a cashier in a department store and, since times were improving, thought she had a good chance of finding that type of employment.

When my mother turned on the radio, we heard the announcer shout, "Pearl Harbor has been attacked by the Japanese." We were almost too shocked to comprehend immediately the meaning of what we were hearing. Our radio stayed on that afternoon as we and our parents hovered around it. Over and over, we heard more reports about the attack by the Japanese. Listening to the radio was the only way we had to get immediate information, for in those days we did not have television, computers, or digital devices. There were newspapers, of course, but even special editions could take hours to show up on newsstands. Most of the radio news that afternoon simply repeated what we'd already heard, but bit by bit we were able to piece together what had happened.

At 7:55 that morning Japanese planes started bombing Oahu and continued the attack throughout the day. Dark clouds of smoke had been reported over the city of Honolulu all morning, and the people who witnessed the attack reported seeing the emblem of the Rising Sun on the wing tips of the planes. It was believed at least fifty planes participated in the attack, and many lives were lost.

As a precaution, Hawaii was put on blackout alert. In the span of a few hours, life had changed forever, not only for Hawaii but for the nation.

I heard my mother say, " I thought they said the war with Germany [that is, World War I] was the war to end all wars."

My father replied, "You know there will always be wars, and rumors of wars. That's what the Good Book says."

The next day, President Franklin D. Roosevelt addressed our nation. He announced that both Manila and Oahu had been attacked by the Japanese. I can still hear his voice as he declared, that the attack was "a date which will live in infamy." Then, on behalf of the United States, he declared war on Japan. I heard the radio broadcast when Mr. Moon, our principal, played it over the grade-school intercom. My sister heard it as well when Principal Verne Hall played it over the high-school intercom.

Germany and Italy were in a mutual-defense pact with Japan, and the U.S. declaration of war against the Japanese prompted them on 11 December 1941 to declare war on the United States. A few hours later, the United States returned the gesture, declaring war on Germany and Italy.

The United States was late to the conflict. The German attack that had precipitated war came more than two years earlier, on 1 September 1939, when Germany invaded Poland. After that, one after another, the countries of the world began a chain of invasions and declarations that by the time of Pearl Harbor saw this lineup: on one side, the United Kingdom, France, Australia, New Zealand, South Africa, Canada, Denmark, Norway, Belgium, Luxemburg, Greece, Yugoslavia, and the Soviet Union; and, on the other side, the so-called Axis Powers of Germany, Japan, and Italy.

We'd been hearing about those countries, and the actions in which they were involved, on the radio for months. But from quiet Sunnyvale it had seemed to be somebody else's conflict, and it had seemed very far away. Now, suddenly, the war had come home, to our home.

California occupied a special place in American war strategies. Along with Oregon and Washington, we were on the front line. The same ocean that washed our shores washed those of Japan, some 5,000 miles away. We seemed vulnerable to the same kind of attack Hawaii had experienced.

We at once understood what this would mean for us, for the very evening that war was declared, we experienced our first blackout. It encompassed the entire San Francisco Bay area. My parents were prepared, and placed dark coverings over our windows. We could hear the humming of planes overhead. We did not know if they were enemy planes, and never really found out. The blackout lasted three hours, and my sisters and I sat silently most of the time, wondering what would happen. The Army soon reported that the planes were indeed enemy planes, but this was quickly denied by the government. Most of the people in Sunnyvale firmly believed the planes were Japanese, and that in denying this the government was simply trying to prevent mass hysteria.

This was just the first of many blackouts during the war, and we soon became accustomed to them.

Within a few days, we began to hear reports that the West Coast was undefended when the Japanese attacked Pearl Harbor. It was said that, if the Japanese government had known, they could have taken the entire area. I don't know if there was any truth to the reports, but I do know it was not long before Army troops moved into our small town.

This was not our town's first experience with government installations. In fact, back in 1931 Sunnyvale actively worked toward the establishment of a local government airbase. It did this by purchasing 1000 acres of farmland bordering San Francisco Bay for almost half a million dollars and then handing the parcel over to the U.S. Government for one dollar. The intention was that the land be used as an airship base. The relatively fog-free location was ideal for this use, and a naval airbase was commissioned NAS Sunnyvale, later renamed NAS Moffett in honor of the rear admiral who'd facilitated the base's original creation. Internal military politics later resulted in Moffett's becoming an Army airbase, used for pilot and air-crew training. At about the same time, in 1935, Ames Laboratory was established at Moffett and became one of the U.S.'s leading research and development centers for aviation-related innovation.

The wartime Army troops were based in several parts of Sunnyvale. The most prominent location was in the area now known as Washington Park, located on Washington and Pastoria Avenues. The land had been purchased by the City of Sunnyvale, and had already been cleared for a park. This was a Godsend, as the land served perfectly for use by our troops. Barracks were quickly built, and the area was transformed into a military complex before our very eyes. Fremont High School also housed some of the troops in one of their buildings. Everyone worked together, and patriotism was paramount.

Our need for this kind of cooperation was demonstrated by the fact that, as early as 11 December, the day we declared war on Germany, the West Coast was identified as a wartime "Western Theatre of Operations" by the Western Defense Command. The roundup of enemy aliens in California, Oregon, and Washington began two days later, netting some 585 Japanese and 187 Germans.

Wartime manpower needs could be quickly met, thanks to the Selective Training and Service Act of 1940, which provided for the first peacetime draft in the United States. Initially, its provisions required that men between the ages of twenty-one and thirty-five register with local draft boards and be subject to military service. After war was declared, the age range for military service was extended to eighteen and forty-five. There was a religious exemption for those who did not believe in war. Many people opposed the 1940 act, while others thought we were getting ready to go to war to support our allies in Europe. Ironically, following the attack on Pearl Harbor, many young men did not wait to be drafted but volunteered for the military. When local boys began to leave home for training, including some who were friends of my sisters, we realized just how close the war had become.

Nine

.. ∘∘●●◗◖∘∘ ..

The Internment of Japanese Americans

Japanese began coming to California and other West Coast states in the late 1860s. They didn't like some of the political changes in their own country and looked to the United States as a place that would offer them more opportunity. Some came as common laborers, but others had enough resources to start businesses.

From the beginning, there was resentment of these newcomers, especially since they were hard workers who often succeeded better than their white neighbors. Attempts were made to undermine their position, including segregation and limitations on land ownership. Early in the twentieth century, the American government negotiated with the Japanese government to discourage the issuance of passports for those wanting to come to America. In 1924 U.S. federal law banned Japanese immigration entirely. This resulted, year by year, in a decrease in the number of American residents born in Japan. Even so, at the time of the Japanese attack on Pearl Harbor, there were still many Japanese or descendants of Japanese living on the West Coast.

We had quite a few Japanese-American farmers in Santa Clara County, and there were Japanese-American businesses as well. For example, what was generally considered to be the best flower shop in the county was owned by Mr. Yonemoto. There were Japanese-American children among my classmates.

After Pearl Harbor, the distrust many white Californians already felt toward their Japanese-American neighbors grew because of the anger toward all things Japanese following the attack. Many whites felt Japanese Americans were loyal to Japan and not the United States. Some went further and called them spies. Rumors even began to circulate around Sunnyvale about Mr. Yonemoto. I remember being told by a neighbor that he had a "regular arsenal" in his home. This was untrue, of course, but many were more than ready to believe it. The people in our town weren't unusual in this regard; Japanese Americans were considered traitors by almost everyone. The popular attitude was quickly incorporated into law.

On 19 February 1942, we were quietly celebrating my father's birthday when we learned President Roosevelt had signed an Executive Order that allowed military commanders to designate "Exclusion Zones" for the approximately 120,000 Japanese Americans living on the West Coast at that time. The Exclusion Zones effectively banned Japanese Americans from miles of coastal areas. The Executive Order also gave authority to the military to have Japanese Americans taken to assembly centers which were quickly set up in California, Oregon, Washington, and Arizona.

The implementation of this Executive Order was harsh. Most of the time those to be interned were notified just two or three days before they had to leave for the assembly centers. They could take with them only their clothes and a few personal belongings. Those who owned their homes were forced either to abandon or sell them for whatever they could get. They either sold their furniture or gave it away. They were forced even to abandon their pets.

I can remember the shock of the grownups and the way small Japanese children cried as they were rounded up. They had no idea where they were moving to, what would happen there, or when they'd be allowed to return, if ever. Many, especially those whose families had been in California for decades, did not understand why this was happening to citizens peacefully going about their business. Even elderly people who'd been brought to the United States as babies over seventy years before were rounded up. Age, occupation, patriotism — none of it made a difference. If they could be identified as Japanese, they were interned.

Ten

· · ·●●◗◖●●· · ·

1942 and Wartime Life

We were living in a nationally difficult time but did not know how difficult. Of course, things had been economically hard for years. My father, who was a sixty-nine-year old cement contractor when the Depression started in 1929, did whatever he could to keep the family afloat in the next decade when very little cement needed to be poured. My mother, thirty-eight years younger, got as much work as she could in the fruit-processing industry. In addition, my parents sold or bartered services and agricultural products for other things we needed. We did not have a car; instead we walked or used public transport. We lived frugally, and my mother knew how to get top value for every penny she spent. She never wore perfume, for example, but dabbed vanilla on her wrist or behind an ear. Even so, during that decade, my father was forced to sell two property lots, on one of which he'd kept his cement mixer in better times.

After the start of the war, national peril increased, but so did community prosperity. Jobs were created because of the war, and people had more money to spend. At the same time many items became hard to buy. Rubber was a scarce product, mainly because of the Japanese conquering Southeast Asia, where our rubber came from. U.S. industry had been producing synthetic rubber for a few years, but it was not as good a commercial product as genuine rubber. Nor did we have the manufacturing capability to produce it on a large scale. Complicating rubber shortages was the fact that the material was needed for military-related equipment. That's probably why the first item rationed by the Office of Price Administration was tires. Gasoline was rationed also, and that helped in limiting the amount of rubber needed for tires and other products. As I mentioned, we did not have a car, but my father had a gasoline cement mixer. Fortunately, in spite of rationing, he always managed to purchase enough gasoline for its operation.

In January 1942, the War Production Board stopped the sale of automobiles to civilians. This left dealers with somewhere around one-half million unsold cars. For a while, cars could be purchased by those in certain occupations, such as the clergy and doctors. In February 1942, the factory production of automobiles was stopped, and the production of war equipment began in earnest. Not long afterwards, the national speed limit was set at thirty-five miles per hour, which helped to conserve both rubber and gasoline.

Rationing affected more than tires and gasoline. In May 1942, every family was issued rationing books holding stamps that could be used for different items. This regulated the quantity of items in short supply that people could buy. Families were particularly affected by the rationing of coffee, sugar, meat, and cooking oil. It wasn't long before canned goods were rationed. This was because the U.S. government had to send canned food to our military and also our allies.

The rationing of sugar was probably the shortage that was most felt by families like ours. We used sugar for our morning cereal and occasional birthday cakes. In the fruit season my mother made jellies or jams, as we had apricot trees and a quince tree in our back yard. I used to help my mother make jelly, and I think that is why I still love making jellies and jams. Unfortunately, jam and jelly recipes called for lots of sugar.

Meat was in short supply, and I remember stores were suspected of selling horse meat. I don't know if that was true, but, even in wartime, no one wanted to buy horse meat. We heard all sorts of rumors throughout the war, and my father would always say: "Consider the source."

My parents were happy when they could purchase a pound of bacon since we always had eggs on hand because we kept chickens. Also, a by-product of cooking bacon became valuable. Meat markets started buying bacon grease along with other cooking fats, and my mother would save the grease by straining it into a one -pound can, which she would take to the butcher shop where it was weighed. She would get extra ration stamps for the grease, which the butcher sold to rendering plants where it was processed into ammunition. One pound of bacon grease would make one pound of dynamite. Bacon grease was also used by pharmaceutical companies in the manufacture of sulfa and other drugs.

During World War II, both butter and margarine were rationed. My mother always bought margarine as it was cheaper than butter. In those days, the government did not allow colored margarine to be sold as it was believed stores would try to substitute it for butter. For that reason, margarine was sold packaged with little packets of color. Housewives would work the powdered color into the soft margarine with a fork, spoon, or any way they could. One day when I came home from school my mother was coloring the margarine. I remember the brand was Nucoa. I asked my mother if I could help her, and I quickly learned it was not easy getting the powdered color worked into the margarine evenly.

Shoes were also in short supply, and rationing stamps were soon issued for them. We were allowed three pairs of shoes a year. If a child outgrew his or her shoes, the rationing board would issue a stamp for another pair.

Rationing and shortages continued throughout the war years. There were also changes in manufacturing related specifically to the need to conserve certain kinds of materials. For example, zippers were not put in clothes. Men's trousers were made without cuffs.

Many items not rationed were in short supply. My sister Marie loved silk stockings, but silk was needed for parachutes. That was when nylon stockings came into the marketplace. Even nylon hosiery became hard to find, and people would line up at stores in San Jose in hopes of purchasing a pair of nylons.

People rarely complained; everyone was willing to sacrifice for the war effort. Maybe that was because we had learned to sacrifice during the 1930s, and doing without was nothing new. Still, it was definitely ironic that people had more money to spend on goods yet could not buy them because they were either rationed or in short supply.

For years, the U.S. government had sold what were known as "defense bonds." After the start of World War II, the name was changed to "war bonds" and the effort to sell them revved up. The price of the bonds was $18.75 with a maturity date of ten years. When matured, the bonds would have a value of $25.00.

This rate of return wasn't as high as you could otherwise get, so the bonds were promoted as a means of investing in the war effort and supporting our soldiers. The bonds were sold in many ways. You could buy them at your job through payroll deduction, for example, or at certain financial institutions. You could buy them on special-purpose occasions, like radio fundraising marathons or sporting events. They were heavily promoted in advertisements, posters, and special publicity campaigns. Artists like Norman Rockwell painted illustrations with the bonds as a theme. Irving Berlin, leading composer of the day, wrote a song called *Any Bonds Today*, which was used as theme music for bond drives. Celebrities, especially movie stars, traveled around the country selling them. Hollywood royalty Carole Lombard, wife of Clark Gable, died while on a bond-drive tour in 1942 when the plane in which she was flying crashed against a mountain near Las Vegas. Ironically, her last film, released after death, was **To Be or Not To Be**, a satire co-starring Jack Benny that made fun of Hitler and the Nazis.

War bonds were also sold in schools, and we students didn't need celebrities to convince us to take part. I was in seventh grade when our teacher Miss Young announced we would have a drive selling the bonds.

"It will be fun to see who can sell the most," she said enthusiastically. "And think of the good you'll be doing."

She gave us the information we needed to sell the bonds and instructed us in the process. We were to sign up purchasers and collect the money, which we were to turn in to the school. The school would then order the bonds. Our class would be recognized for the amount of bonds sold.

That sounded good to us, and we wasted no time. After school that same day, my friend Jackie and I went to the library and sold one bond to Miss Saunders, the librarian. We then went to the home of Mr. Charles Fuller, the owner of Fuller's Camp. Mr. Fuller purchased three bonds, and then we went to the homes of all the people in Sunnyvale whom we knew to be wealthy. We sold eight bonds that afternoon, and the next day we learned we sold more bonds than anyone else in our grade. That felt great!

Students could also purchase stamps for ten cents and up, to be saved in a booklet. When the booklet held enough stamps, we could swap it for a bond. I purchased stamps as did most of my classmates, but I'm not sure how many of us ever had enough to get a bond!

Toward the end of 1942 we started having paper drives at school. There was a small building across the street where we would go and tie the paper in bundles. One day there were five of us, busy tying and having a great time. There was a battery in the room that had been donated for scrap, and a couple of boys started messing around with it, giving each other shocks. One of the boys let out a yell, and soon the principal, Mr. Moon, hurried over to see what was happening. Everyone was quiet by the time he came in the room, and he decided that the shouting had come from somewhere else. The boys were safe that time; and though we often went to the little building to sort papers after that, everyone was more cautious.

Miss Young was also our eighth-grade teacher. Everyone liked her. Not only was she excellent in the classroom, she was a good instructor for our Physical Education classes. We played baseball most of the time, and she thought it would be fun for the girls to play the boys. We had many good players in our class. One boy was Peter Mesa, who later played professional baseball. In some of our games the girls won over the boys. I don't know how that made the boys feel, but we girls were always overjoyed when we won.

In April 1943, we started practicing for our grade-school graduation. Our music teacher had us learn the song *Ah, Sweet Mystery of Life* and memorize the poem *Mrs. O'Reilly*. It seemed to me we practiced that song and poem for two months, and I thought it was a long time. Now, when I look back, I realize it was only one day a week we practiced, so maybe it wasn't so long after all.

Grade-school graduations were always held at the Sunnyvale City Hall as it was larger than our school auditorium, with enough seating capacity so that parents and friends could attend. The City Hall entrance was on Murphy Avenue, and the back of the building was on Frances Street. Our graduations began with a prayer by a pastor from one of the local churches, as that was customary in those days. After we received our diplomas, we were ready for our summer vacation before we started high school. Summer vacation for most of us meant work, play, or a little of both. In these more-prosperous times, it could also mean shopping.

Even when we didn't have a lot of money or it was hard to find exactly what we wanted because of wartime shortages, my girl friends and I enjoyed shopping. Some things we bought locally, but there was a better selection in the shops in San Jose, only a few miles away. To get there, you could take either the train or the bus. The train we caught at the depot. As for the bus, there were three stops in Sunnyvale: on Evelyn and Pastoria Avenues; on Murphy Avenue at Cockrell's News Agency; and at Murphy and the El Camino Highway.

It was convenient to have the pleasant life we lived in Sunnyvale, yet be able to reach a larger, more sophisticated city in just a few minutes by public transport.

Eleven

...•◦•◉◎◉◉◎◉•◦•...

Romance in Wartime

It was Valentine's Day in 1942 when my sister Marie began dating a young Army lieutenant from Mississippi. She went to dances with him at Spanish Hall and to the movies at the local theater or in San Jose. He was soon deployed overseas and she corresponded with him for a period of time until she discovered he was married, when she stopped the correspondence and never spoke of him again.

Marie, an attractive, vivacious girl, had little time to mourn the end of the relationship. She soon met and fell in love with an Army corporal named Bert Coker, also stationed at Washington Park, and on 31 October 1942 they were married.

Shortly after their marriage, Bert was transferred to an Army base in Clovis, New Mexico, where housing was offered for wives. Bert understandably wanted his young wife with him and asked her if she would like to move to New Mexico while he was based there. Marie, as a new bride, was more than willing and left for Clovis on the Greyhound bus to make the 1200-plus-mile journey. Our parents were concerned. Marie, just eighteen at the time, had never been out of California and the long trip was not nonstop but required a transfer. Marie, however, had no apprehensions. There were other girls from Sunnyvale traveling to Clovis at the same time for the same reason as Marie. Recently married, they were joining their husbands in base housing.

Marie, knowing our parents were worrying about her, wrote a short note that she mailed along the way. In it, she assured us that "Traveling by bus is not bad, and I have friends traveling with me."

Reassured, our parents cheered up. My father said, "Marie is friendly, and she will make friends wherever she lives. People are the same everywhere." My mother nodded and replied, "There are good and bad people everywhere, and we all have freedom of choice about those we make our companions. Marie will make the right choice."

Marie was in Clovis only a few weeks, but she wrote home several times. "It is nice here, and I have made a lot of new friends."

We knew she was enjoying herself, and that was all that was important to us.

Bert was soon transferred to the Army base San Luis Obispo which was located in the California city of the same name. Marie returned home, and most weekends Bert had passes to come to Sunnyvale. The chance to see each other that often not only made it nice for them but also helped to relieve some of the pressure of wondering where Bert would be sent next.

In June 1943, he was deployed overseas, to serve under the command of General Patton. When he left, Marie was pregnant. Their son, John Paul, was born 21 January 1944 at the San Jose Hospital. My mother was with Marie when she gave birth.

It was reassuring to have new life appear as the increasingly bloodier war dragged on.

Marie wasn't the only local girl to find a fellow during the war. At Fremont High School, a building was used to train pilots for the military. Also, two military-style Quonset huts were added to the Fremont campus for the training and housing of recruits. As high-school classes still continued, the troops were warned not to fraternize with the students, especially the girls. The girls, however, were inventive. Some would toss note-wrapped rocks onto the football field where the soldiers practiced drills. Some of those notes began or fostered relationships and even marriages.

Dances were held at Sociedad Cervantes Espanola, known as Spanish Hall, and at City Hall, and students and soldiers sometimes mingled there as well. Marie once had me walk her to Spanish Hall, but then I had to go straight home.

Twelve

· · ·●●◖●●● · · ·

Going to High School

In August 1943, I began my freshman year at Fremont Union High School. The school was named after John Fremont, Savannah-born explorer of the West who played a prominent part conquering California in the Mexican Wars. Later, he was one of the first two U.S. senators from California and the first Republican candidate for president.

The school, a beautiful example of Spanish architecture, was much admired. Students from Cupertino and Monta Vista attended the high school along with students from Sunnyvale, and I made many new friends. Fremont was far enough away that we went there by bus, which we boarded at the City Hall or at Washington and Pastoria Avenues. Most of time I got on the bus at City Hall, as that was where most of my close friends boarded.

Jacqueline Stoneberger and Lucille Di Leonardo, friends since first grade, were among those also going on to Fremont. In the summer between grade-school graduation and the start of high school, I made a new friend who has also proved to be enduring, a pretty girl named Mae Miller.

The transition from grade school to high school went very smoothly for me. I especially liked the opportunity we had to choose some of our classes. Some subjects were required, of course: English, Math, Science, and Physical Education. I took Spanish for a foreign language, as we had many Spanish-speaking people living in Sunnyvale. Many of the students taking the course were Spanish; but although they were fluent in the spoken language, they needed to learn how to spell the words correctly. I soon learned I needed to study more for my Spanish class than all the other classes, which I did. I was very competitive, and always wanted to make top grades in all my subjects.

At Fremont, I found that the war was creating new customs. As soon as war was declared, students who were old enough had begun to join the military, and the percentage of boys doing this increased as the fighting continued. When they left for training, the school honored their service by placing a small American flag on their desks. At the graduation services they would have attended had they still been in school, an American flag represented them at their spots on the graduation stand. This affected my sister Edith's classes more than it did mine, but it served to remind all of us of the sacrifices being made on our behalf.

War affected other aspects of life as well. Defense-related manufacturing in the area recruited girls eighteen and over. Since this was the age at which most working girls were employed in the canneries, this created a potential problem.

One evening when I was doing my homework, I heard my parents talking in the living room. My mother seemed worried, and I heard her say, "I don't know what the canneries are going to do this year as most of the eighteen-year old girls have gone to defense plants to work."

My father was quick to reply, "They will think of something. It would not surprise me if they allowed sixteen-year olds to work in the canneries. They have to do something. Our country is dependent on our crops, especially since so much is sent overseas. So, I am positive something will be worked out."

I soon forgot this conversation regarding their idea that sixteen-year-olds would be allowed to work in the canneries. I think that was because I was only fifteen, and the conversation didn't seem to apply to me.

In June 1944, on our last day of school, report cards were handed out, and I was elated. I got high grades in all my classes, and I would be a sophomore the following year. Things got unexpectedly interesting when, shortly before time to go home, we were informed we would have an assembly. We entered the auditorium and were surprised to find that our Principal, Verne Hall, was about to address us. We already knew that he was resigning his position as principal, which I regretted because he was a superb principal. That day, we waited patiently for him to speak; but when he did, I could hardly believe what I was hearing.

"Most of you are aware many of our young people eighteen and older have been hired by defense plants, therefore anyone sixteen years old will be allowed to work in any of the canneries," he announced. "I am handing out work permits and if you would like one just come up to the podium, and I will be glad to issue it."

I watched students line up, one by one. As I was only fifteen, I did not pay much attention at first. Then, I saw a few of my younger classmates get in line. As I watched the principal hand them work permits, little wheels started turning in my head. Given what I'd seen, I knew I could also get a work permit, and I entered the long line. When the assembly was over, with my permit safely in hand, I boarded the school bus for home. My friend Mae Miller lived on Bayview Avenue, about one-quarter mile from Schuckl Cannery, and we immediately hurried over to apply. It was nearing the end of the cherry season, and Schuckl's needed more help canning cherries. We were hired on the spot, but were required to join a labor union in order to work.

We began work the next day, determined to do our best. In fact, the supervisors were afraid we would work too hard. The work was straightforward. The fruit came down to us on a belt, and our job was to pick out overripe cherries and any with stems. We had little bins in which to put the rejects, and then the good cherries would go down the belt to be canned. We did not think the work was hard at all. We had one fifteen-minute break in the morning and one in the afternoon. We had one-half hour for lunch, and we made seventy-five cents an hour, which was the minimum wage in California at that time. We were allowed to work eight hours a day, six days a week. We worked in that department for one week, and then waited at home until the official apricot season began.

Our work with apricots was a little harder than it had been with cherries. We had to cut the apricots, put the seeds in a bin, and then place the apricots on a chute where they would go along a belt to women who sorted them. The apricots then went to the canning department where they were canned. We made a game of the work, as we were competitive. We raced to see who could finish their box of apricots first. Apricot season usually lasted three weeks, and we then had the rest of the summer for other activities.

You couldn't make a fortune working like that, but it was nice to have extra money for personal purposes and also to contribute toward things the family needed. I used some of my earnings to buy school clothes and to go to the movies or skating. What was left, I saved toward Christmas presents.

After cannery season, my friends Jackie and Mae, my sister Edith, and I would go to the movies at Blanco's in Sunnyvale or skating in San Jose. For our roller-skating excursions, we would take a bus to San Jose, and then walk to the rink. We loved skating, and I think we must have skated about fifteen miles each time we went as the roller rink was open three or four hours each evening. We skated to recorded music like *The Skater's Waltz*, wearing our cutest outfits and rented shoes. Across the street from the skating rink, there was a drive-through restaurant where we would board a bus for home. My parents allowed me to go skating as long as Edith was along, as she was two-and-one-half years older and very responsible. Our parents knew we were safe.

It was convenient having older sisters most of the time. I had no surviving younger sister. There had been another girl born after me in 1932 named Molly Jane, but she lived only a couple of weeks because she had a rare skin disease. The slightest touch made her skin peel away, and there was no cure.

I was very young and have no personal memory of Molly Jane's brief time with us. It was only later, in fact, that I even became aware of her existence.

Thirteen

·.₀₀₀oꝊ₀o₀·.

The End in Sight

During my sophomore year at Fremont High, my favorite subject was homemaking. Our fabulous teacher Miss Shank thought everyone should know the art of setting a dinner table.

"Some people just put the silverware down anywhere," she said, "but this is how you do it."

Then she showed us the correct place for all the silverware, plates, cups, and glasses. She was happy only when all her students could set a proper table when she called upon them.

A couple of weeks after school started, we prepared and served lunch for another homemaking class, and they in turn served us. That was fun, and at our luncheon we talked about various subjects. For Laura, one of our classmates, the ongoing war was uppermost on her mind. She said her brother was stationed with the Army in Europe and her family was extremely worried something would happen to him. Miss Shank tried to ease her feelings by talking to her, but nothing seemed to help.

It was hard then not to worry, as it took so long for news to arrive. We did not get reports of happenings almost immediately, as people do today. When we went to the movies, for example, the week's newsreel could be about battles that had happened weeks earlier. Radio broadcasts and newspapers were the only source of information for many people. No one had television in their homes.

One story that topped even the war news was the death of the president. Franklin D. Roosevelt was serving his fourth term when he died on 12 April 1945. When Vice President Harry Truman was sworn in as president, not a lot was known about him. Everyone wondered if he had the ability to lead our country to peace, but less than a month after FDR's death, the war with Germany ended when they unconditionally surrendered on 8 May. Adolf Hitler and many of his close officers were reported to have committed suicide when they recognized the hopelessness of Germany's situation. Most people thought Japan would surrender immediately, but they did not, meaning that the war with Japan continued.

When school ended in June, we were again hired by the cannery. I did not start working that year until the apricot season, and that was fine with me. I could earn money whenever I wanted by babysitting. I could have had a babysitting job every night, but I sat only for a couple of young mothers who lived nearby. I was at the age where I wanted free time for fun things.

That summer, after the apricot season, we were asked to work in peaches. My friend Mae and I worked on the peach machines, and it was not all that hard. Everyone had to wear a hair net, and I remember seeing a sign on the bulletin board that read:

Service men like women's hair, but they don't like to fish it out of cans, so please wear a net.

Everyone laughed when they read the sign. Actually, I don't think anyone ever worked without a hair net, for then as now it was a requirement for working around food.

In August 1945, President Truman authorized the dropping of atomic bombs on Hiroshima and Nagasaki. The devastation was terrible, and on 15 August 1945 Japan surrendered.

The effect on local life was immediate. All defense plants shut down as soon as the war ended. In Sunnyvale, this meant that Westinghouse closed the Joshua Hendy Iron Works (which it had taken over during the war), putting about four hundred workers out of a job. The Westinghouse closure had a trickle-down effect. Many of their workers had moved to Sunnyvale specifically for war work, and now they often returned to their home states. Lela, for whom I often babysat, went back to Missouri, ending the days of easy-to-come-by babysitting money.

Soldiers began coming home, at least those who'd survived the war. Shortages eased, although not immediately. For the first time in almost four years, it was possible for young people to make plans that didn't include wartime conditions.

It was the end of a notable era in Sunnyvale's history and the beginning of a postwar world that would, in many ways, differ significantly from the Depression and war years in which I grew up.

We didn't know that at the time, of course. Even if we had, I doubt it would have mattered. The war was over, and we were ready for life to return to normal.

Fourteen

· ·●●●✪✪●●● · ·

Looking Back

As I re-read the chapters I've written, I wonder what made some events live so vividly in my memory that I felt they must be included in this little book of recollections.

For example, why, in spite of my young age at the time and the fact that we did not personally know the Harts, do I recall the kidnapping and death of Brooke Hart so clearly? It's probably in part because it's been so often talked about in the years since. Four movies and many news stories have been based on the coldblooded murder and the lynching that followed the jailing of its confessed perpetrators. Nationally, what gave the case significance was its treatment as a media event, coupled with the fact that elected officials, including the Governor of the state, had conspired to make the lynching possible.

What I think made the situation matter so much locally was that it was our version of the Lindbergh kidnapping case of the year before. The Harts were both well-known and popular in the community, and the murderers of their son were particularly cruel and callous. In retrospect, I wonder also if there was perhaps an element of frustration that played out in the lynching. The kidnapping had been carried out in an attempt to lay hands on what was then a large amount of money. At a time when almost everyone in the community was experiencing financial uncertainty or hardship, I think there was a great deal of anger that the confessed kidnappers might get away with their financially motivated crime on a technicality even as their law-abiding neighbors were striving to find legitimate work to keep their families afloat.

While my recollection of the details owes something to ongoing news coverage, my memory of the anger in the community is personal and contemporary. Even as a child not quite five, I knew how my parents and their neighbors felt, and it boiled down to their opinion that the Harts were good people who did not deserve to lose their son and the murderers were bad people who deserved to be punished.

As to the lynching, the one public figure who tried to prosecute those responsible for what happened in St. James Park was Alameda County District Attorney Earl Warren, who went on to become Governor of California and, ultimately, Chief Justice of the United States Supreme Court.

Another event that did not directly involve my family but that remains vivid for me is the internment of Japanese Americans during World War II. To this day, it is hard for me to believe American citizens and legal aliens were treated so badly by our government. The anger caused by Pearl Harbor gave those who'd never liked having Japanese in their midst the excuse they needed to get rid of them. Our government's response to Pearl Harbor provided the mechanism for their banishment.

At the time, those of us who had been their classmates, neighbors, and customers did not fully understand what was being done with these Japanese Americans. We knew they were being relocated, but most of us had no idea that they were taken to what amounted to prison camps surrounded by barbed wire. There, they were housed in converted horse stalls and barracks that amounted to little better than shacks. There were ten internment camps, some of them in areas with terrible weather extremes, and no particular efforts were made to protect these citizens turned prisoners from excessive heat and cold. Medical care was often inadequate. More than a few of the prisoners died from physical and emotional stress. Others were killed by armed guards looking for an excuse to shoot anyone they viewed as disobeying orders. The intention of the camps was clearly to punish anyone of Japanese ancestry; even President Roosevelt, who had supported setting up the facilities, called them "concentration camps."

Following the war, most of the Japanese Americans who had lived in Santa Clara County never came back. On a positive note, there was at least one Japanese-American girl in my junior class at Fremont High in 1946. Another classmate who'd been interned did return after the war for a visit, but seemed to have no recollection of the good times that had occurred before her family's relocation.

Some California communities did not want the Japanese-American internees to return. This led many to move to other towns or even other parts of the United States once they were released from the camps.

It was a shameful episode in our national history that has disturbed me increasingly over time.

Clearly, I'm not the only one who continued to feel this injustice long after the war ended. In the 1980s, the U.S. Congress created a commission to review the internment. The commission concluded that it was based on "race prejudice, war hysteria, and a failure of political leadership." Further, it recommended a redress payment to each survivor. Subsequently, President Ronald Reagan signed the Civil Liberties Act of 1988, apologizing for Japanese-American internment and providing for $20,000 reparations per person.

Mostly, when I look back at my growing-up years, of course, what I remember best is home and the much-loved people who lived there. I recall fondly the Depression Glass of which my mother was so proud and am glad to know she lived to see it become valuable to collectors. I picture the pretty dresses she made for me and my sisters and wish I had her sewing talent. I think of the warm, affectionate family situation she and my father managed to create for us in spite of all the economic challenges and wartime uncertainties.

Most of all, I think of how, even now, my life is enriched by lessons they demonstrated in their lives. Some of what they taught us is "big-picture" stuff — a good work ethic, always giving value for money, generosity toward those less fortunate, kindness toward animals, bravery when facing the future. I can't help wondering, however, if the "small things" are any less important. To take just one example, the hours I spent with my mother making jelly and the pleasure that I saw everyone take in the result set a precedent for the rest of my life. I still love making jellies and jams. I always have a few jars on hand for my family and friends. Each part of that process, the preparation and the sharing, even now reminds me of Mother and the many ways she expressed her love and concern for us and for others.

I think another lesson, taught as much by the times as by any particular family example, was the importance of savoring what you have, even if it isn't exactly what you want. Growing up in the Depression, there were many things my sisters and I wanted and could not have: all the toys we saw advertised; store-bought dresses; fancier shoes; endless money for movies and skating; and the ability to travel. Most of all, we would have liked for our parents to have it easier or, at least, to get more reward for all their hard work. In spite of that, we were happy, happy with our parents, with each other, and with our town.

Everything changes. In the years since the end of World War II, most of the family members with whom I shared that time have sadly died. As for Sunnyvale, the town that all of us knew, it is transformed. I moved away long ago and was overwhelmed on a recent visit by the evolution of the place in the years since my childhood.

Before I did anything else, I wanted to go by the house on West Washington Avenue where I was born and grew up. As I drove down the avenue, I noticed that the grade school I attended was no more, its place now taken by a shopping mall. As I drew nearer to our old address, I saw that many of the houses I remembered from the past have been replaced by newer residences. That has also been the fate of my childhood home. At our old address is a Mission-style house, attractive and almost certainly equipped with the latest conveniences. I'm sure the people who live there find it a welcoming refuge, just as our family found our more-modest dwelling. Still, it saddened me. I've lived long enough to know that the years bring alterations we can only accept with a greater or lesser degree of grace, but it was still hard for me to see that our house is gone.

On the other hand, some things I had thought temporary are still around. During World War II, when there was an urgent need to house soldiers as quickly as possible, Quonset huts were erected near the Boys' Gym at Fremont High School. To my surprise, they are still there, used for school purposes now.

Still, in the decades since I left, more has changed in Sunnyvale than has remained the same. As I drove through streets I'd known in childhood as well as I knew our own yard, I saw that the once-sleepy town surrounded by fruit orchards is now a thriving metropolis with little sign of the past that I remember. It seemed so unbelievable to me that I felt like Rip Van Winkle waking from a long sleep. A feeling of nostalgia swept over me, a feeling I could not dismiss, not nostalgia for the hard times we lived through but for the place and people I knew.

As to those hard times, I'll share something my father often said: "If you have never tasted the bitter, you won't enjoy the sweet."

The End

Elsie's Family Album

My Grandparents

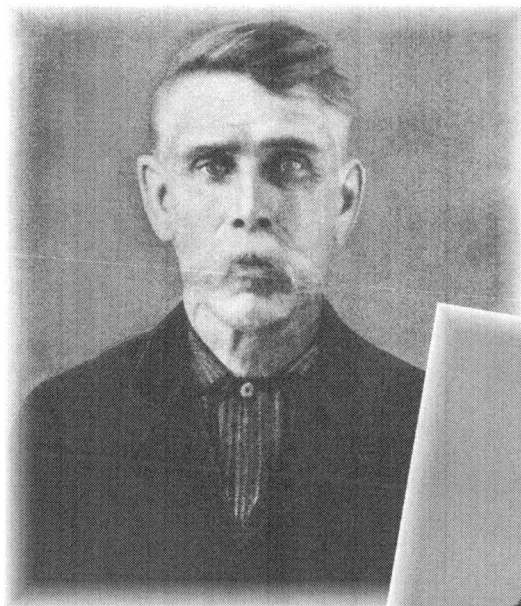

At Left is Henry Daley McCain (1836-1907), my father's father. There are no known photographs of his wife, Margaret Cornelia Mosteller, who died in 1884.

Above is my mother's father, Robert Robinson (1856-1922), who abandoned the family when she was a little girl.

At left is my mother's mother, Eve Laney (1872-1950).

My Parents When Young

At left is my father Columbus McCain (1860-1947), at the age of twenty.

Below are Sarah Robinson (1893-1929), my mother's older sister, and - at right - my mother Martha Jane Robinson (1898-1984), at the age of two.

My Parents in the Year of Their Marriage

This photograph was taken in 1923, the year of my parents' marriage. In the top row are my mother, Martha Jane Robinson (1898-1984), and my father, Columbus Van Buren McCain (1860-1947). In the front row is Julia Pearl McCain (1904-1939), one of my father's six children by his first wife Julia Elmira Watts (1860-1919), together with her husband Marshall Smith (1901-1980). My mother's family lived in the house next door to my father, and my mother was engaged to another man at the time she noticed the handsome, older widower. She broke the engagement and let herself be courted by my father. As for the beautiful Pearl, she later died in a mysterious fire.

Our Family in the 1930s

An itinerant photographer took the photograph, below, of my sisters and me in a goat cart at the start of the 1930s. My sister Edith (1926-2009) is at the left. My sister Marie (1923-2007) is at the right. I'm in the middle, helping to hold the reins. I'm looking uncertain, and the goat looks bored with it all. Notice the stockings. Mother had a strict rule about little girls wearing long stockings, which was irritating because they kept sliding down.

On the opposite page are our parents, Our father, Columbus Van Buren McCain (1860-1947) was seventy-four when this photograph was taken in 1934. Our mother, Martha Jane Robinson (1898-1984) was around thirty-six when this photograph was taken circa 1935. In spite of the difference in ages, theirs was a genuine love match, and each wholeheartedly supported the other in keeping our family healthy and secure during the dark days of the Depression.

Our Little Girl Pictures

Above are, at left,
Marie (1923-2007)
and Edith (1926-2009),
circa 1928.

At left, I'm posing
in the garden,
circa 1931.

Me at Eight
And the Christmas Ring

Above, I'm in the yard
of our house at Sunnyvale,
circa 1937.

At right is the birthstone
ring my mother got for me
that special Christmas
with Crystal White Soap
wrappers. My sisters each
got one too. We were thrilled.

High School
At Last

My Sister Marie
In 1942

This photograph was taken around the time that Marie (1923-2007) was married to a soldier based at Washington Park in Sunnyvale.

My Father and
One of His Grandsons

In this photograph, my father, Columbus Van Buren McCain (1860-1947), is shown at our house in Sunnyvale with Dale Ashby (1923-2009), the youngest child of Georgia Alice McCain (1883-1965), the second daughter of his 1880 marriage to Julia Elmira Watts (1860-1919).

My New Outfit

Here I am, circa 1944, wearing the saddle shoes and coat I bought with money I earned the summer before. A lot of us kids worked sorting or processing fruit in part of the summer vacation to earn money. I loved those shoes.

Girls Together

I'm at left and Mae Miller is at right, circa 1945.

I'm at left and a girl named Ruby is at right, circa 1944.

You did a lot with your girl friends when I was growing up. You hung out with them at school, When you were little, you played together after school. When older, you went shopping, skating, and to the movies together. You even worked together during summer vacations. If you were lucky, as I have been, you keep some of them as friends all your life.

Below, in a photograph taken circa 1944, I'm with several girl friends. I'm at right in the top row, next to Mae Miller. In the bottom row are Frances Yglesias, Jacqueline Stoneberger, and Lucille Di Leonardo.

Fun Times

Lucille Di Leonardo and I were playing croquet at Fremont High when this was taken, circa 1944.

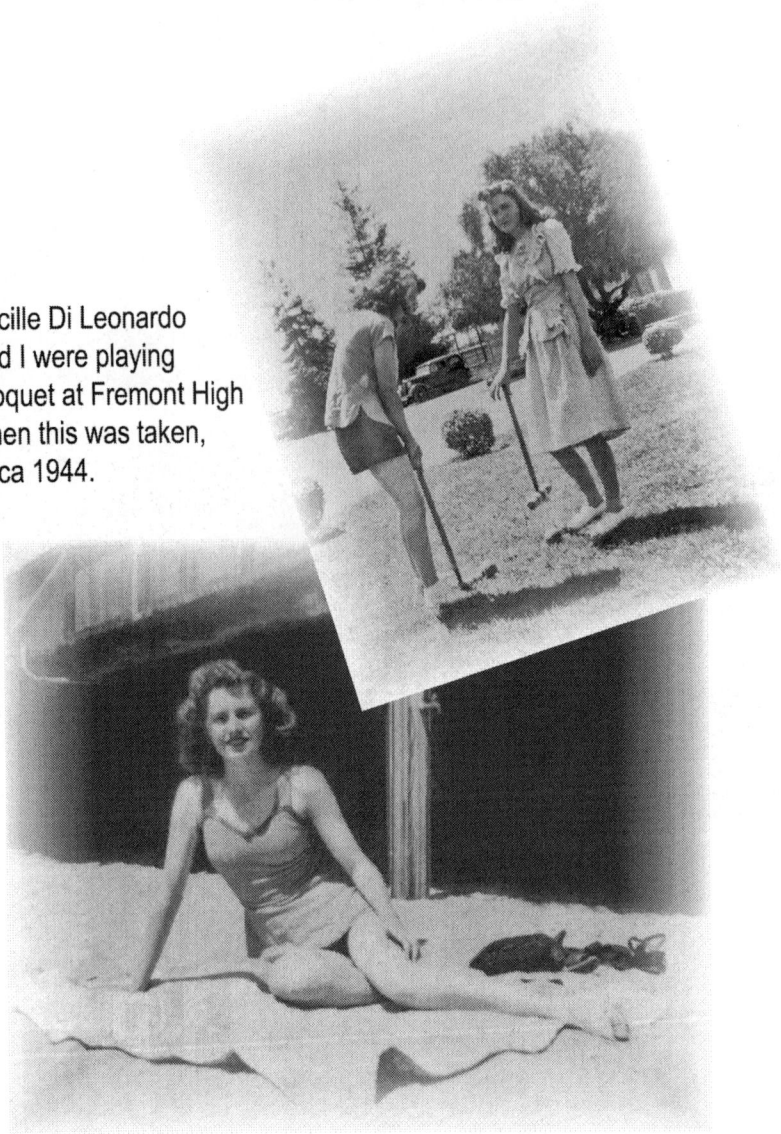

Sunnyvale is only a few miles from the Pacific Ocean, and my friends and I went over whenever we could. Above, I'm relaxing at the beach on a hot day, circa 1946.

Fremont High School Junior Picture

This is a section of the 1946 Fremont High School Junior Picture.
I'm the third from the left, in the second row from the top.

My Parents
in the 1940s

My Father and My Nephew

Here's my father Columbus Van Buren McCain (1860-1947), holding his grandson John Paul Coker (born 1944), son of my sister Marie (1923-2007) and her husband Bert Coker (1920-1990). Date is circa mid-1945.

Growing Up

Ready to Launch

Jacqueline Stoneberger, at left, and my sister Edith, at right, with me in the center, posing in the parking lot at the railroad station. It was a happy time.

Acknowledgments

·₀·₀₀●**❋❋**●₀₀·₀·

I want to give thanks to my wonderful parents who toiled end-less hours to provide my sisters and me with daily necessities when the economy was at its most challenging. Their devoted love has remained with me throughout my life.

I am thankful to my sisters for the memories of precious times we had together. We were like the three musketeers, always sharing and caring for each other.

I give thanks also to my childhood friends Lucille Di Leonardo, Mae Miller, and Jacqueline Stoneberger for the fun and experiences we shared. We have journeyed through the difficult days of the Great Depression, World War II, and beyond. This book would not have been complete without those memories.

The writing of this book has been an extraordinary adventure for me. I want to thank Linda Hewitt, my Mosteller second cousin once removed, for the encouragement and support she has given me throughout and also for the time and effort she has spent in the book's editing.

Thanks also to my cousin-in-law Robert Hewitt for his expertise in designing the book's cover and his help in the layout of my photo album.

Finally, I must acknowledge the inspiration provided by my children, grandchildren, great-grandchildren, nieces, and nephews. Knowing that they may find interest and possibly even pleasure in reading about the lives we lived in long-ago Sunnyvale has been my greatest spur.

∘ ∘ ●●◐◐●● ∘ ∘

Book Notes

Colophon

The cover design for *California Girl: Growing Up in the Great Depression* is by Robert Hewitt. The book is laid out in Adobe InDesign CC. The body is set in Adobe Garamond Pro, the chapter names in Chalkduster, and the chapter numbers in Brinar Bold. The chapter ornaments are Ann Dividers.

Issue and Edition Notes

California Girl: Growing Up in the Great Depression is available as a Kindle edition and trade paperback.

Rights Information

California Girl: Growing Up in the Great Depression is copyrighted, with all rights reserved to the author. For rights information, email rights_info@elsiewhite.net.

∘ ∘ ●●◐◐●● ∘ ∘

Made in the USA
San Bernardino, CA
14 July 2015